THE MAGIC WORKSHOP

A resource for anyone who works with young people in a creative and fun way

D1610738

Written and illustrated by
THOMAS MOLONEY

Russell House Publishing

First published in 2006 by:
Russell House Publishing Ltd.
4 St. George's House
Uplyme Road
Lyme Regis
Dorset DT7 3LS

Tel: 01297-443948
Fax: 01297-442722
e-mail: help@russellhouse.co.uk
www.russellhouse.co.uk

British Library Cataloguing-in-publication Data:
A catalogue record for this book is available from the British Library.

ISBN: 1-903855-92-6
       978-1-903855-92-8

Also by the same author: *Golden Hours: Games for Groups* (RHP, 2003)

Printed by Alden Press, Oxford
Photographs by Landy Photography

About Russell House Publishing

RHP is a group of social work, probation, education and youth and community work practitioners and academics working in collaboration with a professional publishing team.

Our aim is to work closely with the field to produce innovative and valuable materials to help managers, trainers, practitioners and students.

We are keen to receive feedback on publications and new ideas for future projects.

For details of our other publications please visit our website or ask us for a catalogue. Contact details are on this page.

Contents

FOREWORD

By Quentin Reynolds

Congratulations! You have in your hands a real magic book. This book can help you bring magic into the lives of thousands of children and young people. It will bring not just the magic of tricks but the magic of fun, laughter and a sense of accomplishment. Not many books can do that.

Having worked in children's entertainment for twenty-five years I have a notion of what children like. There's no doubt that partaking in *The Magic Workshop* will be a memorable event for every child. I would love to have attended something like this when I was a boy.

This workshop gives every child the chance not just to participate and learn, but to take away something that they can later show to their friends and relatives. It allows them to explore their curiosity and creativity.

As I read through *The Magic Workshop* it dawned on me that this is not just for children. It could also form the basis of a creativity workshop for adults. Thomas Moloney has made splendid decisions in his choice of material. Some of the items can be made more challenging if you wish.

He has also provided all the raw materials for you. If you plan on giving a lot of workshops you can have the materials printed up in bulk. Do shop around and get quotes from different printers. You'd be surprised just how much prices can vary. Get samples of the card or paper they will use for printing and check if they meet your requirements before giving the go-ahead.

Thomas is giving you a complete plan with all the hints and tips he has learned from his own experience. Don't just skim over this, read it through a few times so that you get a full mental image of how you should present the workshop. Don't be afraid to make your own notes on the pages.

Consider the venues in which you can present *The Magic Workshop*. There are the obvious ones like schools, libraries and youth centres. There are also church groups, girl guides, scout groups, arts festivals and summer camps to consider. As mentioned earlier, I can also see this as a creativity workshop for adults. Wouldn't senior groups enjoy this? It would give them something to show their grandchildren.

Before you give your first workshop invite a dozen of your adult friends over for an afternoon and conduct the workshop with them. Seriously! I guarantee that you and they will have immense fun. You should also listen to their comments. Doing this will give you tremendous feedback and possibly even a few jokes or funny comments that will add to your presentation.

Whether you're a youth worker, a teacher or a magician you have in your hands a book full of tremendous possibilities. Whether you just want to use the material once or twice, or set up a part-time business, the option is yours. This is a book that allows you to lead an activity, which will bring you immense satisfaction, provide great fun for the participants and add to your bank account! Yes, that is real magic!

Quentin Reynolds spent 25 years as a full-time children's entertainer during which he presented his own children's TV show *Quentin's Magic* on RTE, Irish television. His shows featured magic, Punch and Judy, ventriloquism and the big secret: tons of audience involvement. More recently he has spent his time teaching other children's entertainers how to get the maximum reaction from their shows. He is now based in the United Kingdom.

Introduction

This book is the result of ten years of work exploring the potential of using the art of magic as a developmental tool in working with young people.

As a professional youth worker and art teacher I have always been examining innovative and creative ways of engaging with young people. I have aimed to identify inclusive, non-competitive approaches such as co-operative games, drama and art. Traditionally, sport and competitions have been popular with leaders working with young people. Although such activities can be enjoyable and developmental for the participants, they are of little benefit to those who are not into competitive sport. In recent times, there has been a growing awareness of the need for non-competitive and creative approaches in the realm of youth work. The main reason for this is that many young people feel intimidated, and excluded, by competition. It is therefore important that other avenues of interest be explored and made available to be used as effective methods of engagement within this sphere of work.

Youth work is about enabling the young person to grow. This happens in an informal way and is dependent on establishing good relationships. The role of the youth worker is to journey with the young person and to enable them to gain the knowledge, attitudes and skills necessary to meet their developmental needs.

The inspiration for the Magic Workshop emanated from my interest and many years of involvement in magic. As a child, like most other children, I was fascinated by magic. As I grew older I began to learn the methods and techniques used by magicians and as my knowledge increased I began performing magic. My teaching job took me into numerous classrooms working with hundreds of kids so it was inevitable that magic would come to the fore. I enjoyed performing magic in the classroom and of course the kids were delighted to see such strange deeds during their work times. The magic was an attention grabber. The kids became more engaged in the subject being taught, performed better, were more creative and most importantly were having fun. Gradually I began to realise that magic was more than just an amusing entertainment.

My use of magic as a means of working with young people further evolved as a result of my collaboration with fellow magician Ger Godley who actually created the framework concept for the Magic Workshop. Ger is a professionally trained youth worker and for twelve years was manager of a regional youth service. He always had a particular interest in exploring creative ways of working with young people. Over the years he has experimented with a variety of approaches including drama, art, music, circus skills, photography and co-operative games. With his interest in magic it was logical that he would incorporate it into his work with young people. His competence as a youth worker, experience as a trainer and knowledge of magic added greatly to the subsequent development of the workshop.

The Magic Workshop has become a popular attraction in schools, clubs, festivals and summer camps and now forms a sizeable portion of my annual professional engagements.

It is important to clarify that the Magic Workshop is not about teaching the secrets of magic. Instead its purpose is to use magic as a means of engaging with young people and enabling them to view themselves as increasingly capable and competent in their communication and social skills with far reaching consequences in the development of the young participants.

The Magic Workshop has a number of elements that lends itself to quality youth work:

- The young person is affirmed.
- The workshop has the potential to respond to such needs as self-confidence, communication skills, sense of achievement and being acknowledged.
- The workshop is not a 'sit and watch' event. It is a learning experience that involves full participation and interactivity for each person.
- The participants learn new skills, have opportunities to perform for others and also get to teach others. Opportunity is also provided for the young people to introduce some of their own ideas.
- Lots of opportunity is provided for conversation and discussion.
- The varied programme of the workshop helps the participants to explore their creative sides.
- All the participants have fun.

A considerable amount of thought and work has gone into the content and design of this book to make it as complete and as self-contained as possible. It contains a bulk of information and resource material that will enable you to deliver successful magic workshops. The book is divided into two main parts. Part 1 describes the necessary preparation and how to present the workshop. Part 2 is the resource section and contains the warm-up games, group focusing activities, tricks and give-aways all arranged in separate categories. All these ideas have been thoroughly tried and tested. Prior knowledge of the art and skill of magic is not necessary. All materials required for the workshop are clearly described. Templates and instructions are supplied for the various tricks and puzzles you will need to make.

Using this book

How you choose to use this book is up to you. It is not necessary to deliver the workshop exactly as outlined. In fact, it is recommended that you shape the contents to your own style and the needs of the young people you are working with. Although I have been presenting the workshops for several years I have rarely delivered any two that were identical. The age group, size of the group, workspace, time and resources available all determine the shape of the workshop.

Alternatively, you may decide to just pick one or two of the ideas contained herein and use them in a one-off experience. Many of the activities can be used as effective icebreakers, energisers or simply as a means of initiating conversation.

You could also choose to organise a number of workshops over a period of time and work towards an event where the participants put on a performance.

Who this book is for

The ideas in this book should be of benefit to anyone interested in working with young people in a developmental way. Group leaders, teachers, club organisers, trainers, counsellors, informal educators and children's entertainers should find something in here that they can use in their work with any age group.

Magicians and children's entertainers

This book should be of special interest to magicians, and other children's entertainers, who may wish to facilitate workshops for young people on the art of magic. The Magic Workshop can also be used to attract extra professional engagements for the working magician who may tailor the idea to suit a one-off event or develop a series of workshops over a longer period of time. The fact that the Magic Workshop creates a novel angle for using magic as an educational tool, together with its suitability for all age groups, opens up the largely untapped market of the older child and teenager for the entrepreneurial entertainer.

Youth workers, group leaders and informal educators

Youth workers, group leaders and informal educators should find here several innovative ways to engage with young people. Puzzles, tricks and magic hold a fascination for young people of all ages. Obviously, different presentations are required for different age groups. The Magic Workshop can be presented as detailed or changed to suit any type of group situation.

Teachers

Teachers can use many of these ideas in the classroom environment to help stimulate interest and enthusiasm for the lesson in progress. All teachers know that boredom can easily set in during a class period so keeping the attention of students is vital for a successful lesson. Students can't learn if they aren't paying attention. If the students know that something unusual or funny might happen at any moment, they are more liable to pay attention. As a classroom teacher, I can testify to the fact that the performance of magic tricks greatly enhances the students' interest and can turn a seemingly monotonous lesson into an exciting and memorable experience.

I have gained so much in so many ways from the success of the Magic Workshop and I know that you too, with a little effort, can use this book in your work to help you to do the same. Take these ideas, make them your own and create a special kind of magic in every sense of the word.

Thomas Moloney

Thomas Moloney is a member of the International Brotherhood of Magicians (IBM) and has presented 'Tommy's Magic Workshop' in countless schools, clubs, festivals, summer camps etc. over a ten-year period. He is also an art teacher and youth worker and uses games, art and magic to deliver engaging workshops to young people and adults in schools, clubs and leader-training programmes. His other book, *Golden Hours: Games for Groups* is a collection of games and exercises for groups of all ages and sizes and is also available from Russell House Publishing.

Acknowledgements

I wish to sincerely thank the following people and organisations for their assistance in bringing this project to fruition:

- Ger Godley, fellow magician, for his professional information and expertise, both in magic and in youth work, throughout the project.
- Mary Fagan for her suggestions, tips and much appreciated help.
- Staff of the Kerry Diocesan Youth Service for organising the group for the photographs and particularly the kids for their patience and willingness to participate.
- Russell House Publishing Ltd. for publishing another one of my manuscripts.
- And of course the countless kids who made the magic by attending the magic workshops throughout the years.

Part 1

Preparing and Presenting
The Magic Workshop

An attractive aspect of the Magic Workshop is that, aside from the materials for the workshop and your own skill as a facilitator, little else is needed. A large room or hall to accommodate the group and which allows space for working in smaller groups is all that is required. You do not even need chairs or tables.

Preparing for the Magic Workshop

Before delivering the Magic Workshop, a certain amount of preparation is needed. All preparation should be carried out well in advance so that you are focused and relaxed when you meet the group. This not only means having all the materials ready but also knowing what you are going to do and what you are going to say. You will need to gain some information about the group that you will be working with, such as the size of the group and the average age of the participants.

An ideal group size for the workshop is sixteen. You can of course work with less or more. If the group is over sixteen it is recommended that you involve a second facilitator. The task of this person is to help out with managing the group. They do not necessarily need to have knowledge of the content of the workshop. Most groups will have their own leaders and helpers anyway.

Knowing the age of the participants is important. The various tricks in this book are ability coded from Level 1 to Level 3. You should use this code to help you to decide which items are appropriate for the particular group you are going to work with. This will ensure that you have a trick to suit the ability of each member of the group.

When making up the tricks, make up enough for each participant. The tricks have been specially selected and developed so that all you need to do for most of them is photocopy your preferred ones onto card.

It is essential that you become familiar with all the tricks and games in advance. Familiarity breeds confidence. Learn and practice the tricks. This may sound like a chore but it can be a lot of fun. Only when you can confidently perform a trick should you use it in the workshop. To introduce a trick that you are uncertain about will greatly lessen the impact of the trick and the effectiveness of the objective of your workshop.

Checklist

The following is a checklist of all the items you need during the magic workshop and what you need to do to get ready, and out the door.

Briefcase

A briefcase or small bag will be necessary to transport the various items and copies you will need for the Magic Workshop.

Tape or CD player

Music is a desirable ingredient in creating the pre-workshop atmosphere and may also be used during the games. A tape or CD player is therefore a valuable asset to the presentation of the workshop.

Try to use one with a remote control facility, as this will allow you to move around the hall while a game is in progress.

Labels and markers to make name tags

Labels are perfect for making name tags. I use a roll of self-adhesive address labels that are available at any good stationery store. Also take a couple of markers with you. On arrival at the venue, give the whole lot out

to the club leaders to put a name on each participant. This saves a lot of hassle and allows you to get your own preparation done more swiftly.

Trick cards for the swap-around warm-up game

These can be found in the Warm-up Activities Section on page 29. Just follow the instructions on how to make them up for the game, and then pop them into your workshop bag.

Puzzles

A puzzle will be used to focus the group during the workshop. Choose one from the Group Focusing Activities Section on page 41 and follow the instructions to prepare this for the workshop. Again, put this into your workshop bag.

Workshop tricks

These are the tricks that you will use during the workshop presentation. They can be found in the 'Tricks' Section on page 59. Follow the advice given on choosing tricks related to the ability of your group. For most of the tricks, all you'll need to do is photocopy them and cut out the trick's cards. Others will require a simple easily found item.

Give-away pack

Follow the advice on how to make up The Magic Workshop Give-away pack on page 101. You will need to make up one for each participant in your workshop.

Last thoughts

Make sure to include **contact phone numbers** for your client and **address details of the venue** in your workshop bag. You never know when you will really need to contact your booker if you get lost or are delayed due to unforeseen circumstances.

Now, you should be ready to go!

At the Venue

The importance of timing

Start on time and finish on time. A timetable prepared in advance can be of great help. It enables you to structure the session and to avoid rushing at the end because of delaying too long on a particular activity. If, however, your planned timetable is not working do not hesitate to abandon it and improvise.

It's wise to give yourself some time prior to running the workshop to check out the facilities available and to make sure that you are ready to give your full attention to working with the group when the time comes. Being calm and relaxed as the participants enter the room will ensure that you have few issues of discipline or of creating the right atmosphere.

If, however, you arrive late and find the participants hanging around frustrated, you will not have time to properly set up the room. You will also find it very difficult to recover as the workshop proceeds. Make life easier for yourself and the workshop more enjoyable for the participants by arriving on time. You can then easily complete all preparations and be relaxed and ready to focus on the running of the workshop.

Creating the atmosphere

It is important to create a calm and pleasant atmosphere from the beginning. The room or hall should be free of clutter. There should be a sense of the participants entering a space that is different.

With the use of the CD player, music can help to create this atmosphere. Playing some fast-paced circus type music as people gather can create a sense of fun and expectation. Failing this, some lively, popular music would suffice.

A colourful sign outside the door announcing the workshop can also help set the mood. The important thing is to create an atmosphere to communicate that this will be different, interesting and also professional. Giving a little thought to this aspect at the beginning can set a pleasant tone for the whole workshop.

From the moment the participants enter the room you should communicate an air of relaxation, fun and friendliness. Acknowledge and informally welcome them as they enter. Introduce yourself and the other leaders. Speak clearly. Engage with the group in a pleasant manner communicating both a sense of confidence and competence. If you have a good memory you should learn the first names of all the participants. Provide them with markers and labels to make name tags.

Having the names of participants visible on their person not only makes it easier for you to speak to the members; it is also an excellent group trust-developing procedure.

Most people feel more relaxed around people whose names they know. The name label also helps to open up lines of communication between the participants. Remember that one of the sweetest sounds a person can hear is the sound of their own name. Participants will respond positively and be more co-operative when referred to by their first names. Successful sales people use this technique all the time.

Take the time to talk with individual participants as they arrive. This is not only basic common courtesy but also a clever warm-up technique. Note, I say talk *with* them, not *at* them. Don't talk about what is going to happen during the workshop or about yourself and your status. Instead converse about anything else – the weather, cars, television programmes, music, books, aeroplanes etc. It may not seem important to do this but I guarantee you that this little chit-chat is a wonderful way to create a relaxed pre-workshop atmosphere.

Other tips to bear in mind

Focus on the process rather than the product
In developmental group work it is the journey to achieving the outcome that matters. All participants will not progress at the same speed so do not rush. Show respect to all involved, encourage each member to participate and congratulate them on their efforts as well as their achievements.

Have fun
Join in the action and have fun with the group. Be enthusiastic in your presentation. Also remember that a smile goes a long way towards creating a good atmosphere in a group. Do not hesitate to show the group that you enjoy what you do. Your enthusiasm will be contagious.

Listen

Become a listener. Listen actively to what the participants are telling you. Remember that listening involves more than paying attention to what is being said. It also involves being aware of body language and the atmosphere within the group. Good leaders are excellent listeners and have heightened awareness skills.

When working with groups:

Do not embarrass

At no time should you humiliate or embarrass a participant. Pay attention to the manner in which you address the group and avoid any comments or actions that may cause offence. Also respect a member's right not to participate in a particular activity. There may be some imperceptible reason for the unwillingness such as an illness, an injury or some other discomfort.

Do not act the expert

Your approach to working with the group members should be one of enabling and empowering them to learn for themselves. As a facilitator, your job is not to provide a 'one right answer' but rather to direct the participants to discover a whole range of answers themselves.

Do not work on your own

When working with children always have another adult present. Also remember it is imperative to ensure that a safe environment is created for young people accessing any kind of workshop or youth service.

Do not lose control

At all times remain calm and composed even when something goes wrong. If you behave in a manner that communicates competence and proficiency then the group members will have confidence in you as a facilitator.

Do not exclude people

Work in an inclusive manner making sure that all feel welcome and valued. Each person is important and contributes to the life of the group.

Do not confuse

Communicate in a clear fashion and avoid confusion or vagueness. Encourage participants to ask questions when they are unsure and be prepared to demonstrate an action to illustrate a point.

Presenting The Magic Workshop

AN OVERVIEW OF THE MAGIC WORKSHOP

4 Learning a magic trick
In small groups each participant learns a trick.

5 Performing their tricks
Opportunity is provided for each person to perform their trick.

3 Puzzle time
In small groups the participants are given a group challenge that is lots of fun.

6 Teaching each other new tricks
The participants share with each other the secret of their trick and how to perform it.

2 Fun game with a magical theme
Encourages participants to move around, greet others, have a laugh. Concludes with magical surprise.

7 Large group activity
Entertainment and fun for the entire group OR a group game OR Make and Do.

1 Welcome
Participants are welcomed and invited to partake in some fun, puzzles and mystery.

8 Distribution of Magic Packs
Each participant is given a pack with all the tricks that were taught at the workshop.

"START"

"END"

Welcome

It is important to get the group involved as quickly and easily as possible. If this is a new group, the members will naturally look to you, as the leader, for direction and support.

At this stage you will be the centre of attention so it is essential to model the type of behaviour that you feel is suitable for the running of your workshop.

It is better not to spend too much time talking here. My advice is to get started as swiftly as possible. Begin by welcoming the participants, briefly introduce yourself and any other leaders present, and then immediately get into the warm-up activity.

Warm-up activity

2

Fun game with a magical theme
Encourages participants to move around, greet others, have a laugh. Concludes with a magical surprise.

Movement usually captures people's attention. Warm-up activities are ideal for this purpose as they help the participants to feel more comfortable with themselves and with each other. They also help to develop the kind of atmosphere that creates an enthusiastic and willing group.

The Warm-up Games Section contains games suitable for this part of the workshop. One game in particular, The *Swap-around Game*, was especially created for the Magic Workshop concept and is well worth the preparation required.

The type of warm-up activity used in the Magic Workshop should ideally conclude with the group divided into smaller groups of three or four participants. Make sure each group has its own space and then request them to sit on the floor. The groups are now ready for the *focusing* stage.

Focusing the group

3
Puzzle time
In small groups the participants are given a group challenge that is lots of fun.

Following the warm-up activity, which ended with the group divided into three, four or five smaller groups, there is now a new situation for the participants. They may or may not know each other. If they do, they may not have all worked together before. Different group arrangements produce different dynamics and you need to be aware of this as you proceed through the workshop.

For you, the leader, there is also another concern. You now want to present the tricks to the groups but cannot possibly get to each group at the same time (unless you are a real magician!). Plus you want to keep the momentum of the workshop going during this stage.

What is required here is a group-focusing activity – something to get each group's members actively involved and working together. This also has the added advantage of keeping them occupied whilst you visit the various groups.

Puzzles are ideal for this time. Each group gets the same puzzle. The puzzle that you use must be challenging but not impossible. A suitable puzzle is one that looks achievable, has few pieces and benefits from combined brain power. They know the answer is there but it seems just beyond their reach, like the proverbial carrot in front of the donkey.

In my experience, young people have a tremendous interest in puzzles and problem solving exercises. They really get into them with incredible persistence and this gives you the freedom to move around to each group with the selected tricks.

Presenting the magic tricks to the group

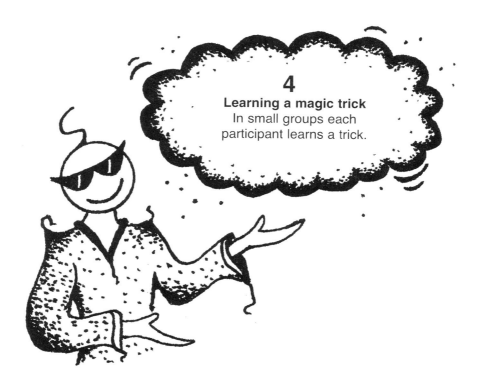

4
Learning a magic trick
In small groups each
participant learns a trick.

The groups are now actively engaged in trying to solve the puzzle. This is the time to present the workshop tricks to them.

- When you approach a group with a magic trick, the first thing to do is gain the attention of each member of this group. One or two may be so interested in the puzzle that you'll actually need to say 'OK, let's forget the puzzle for the moment, you may go back to it later, but I need to give you a special trick now.'
- Having obtained everyone's attention, request that they watch closely as you present the trick to them. The trick will really capture their interest.

- Next explain how it works. Spend some time showing them the handling that is necessary to successfully perform the trick.
- Then give one copy of the trick to each member of this group. Inform them that they'll need to spend the next few minutes practising it so that they can show it to others later. Request them to stay in their own group and not to move about the hall until you give the signal.
- Now move onto the next group with a different trick and repeat the same procedure.
- When you have presented a trick to all the groups, visit each group again, briefly, to check their understanding and ability to do the trick. Give some time to those that need additional help and explanation.

You are now ready for the next stage.

Notes

- Sometimes, during your presentation of a trick, the kids will say that they know how the trick is done. Don't be put out by these remarks. Just continue by saying *'That's good because you'll be showing this trick to the other groups soon'*.
- If a participant tells you that a trick is stupid, read the situation. There may be a number of reasons why that comment was made. Anyway, you can continue with the same trick by saying *'That's what I thought too, but look, it's actually very clever! Watch…'*
- It's important to present the tricks without an attitude of smugness.

Splitting and forming new groups

The next stage of the Magic Workshop is to create a situation whereby the participants who have just learned a new trick can show this to others who haven't seen it. This is a very powerful time in the Magic Workshop. It is where the basics of communication, co-operation and trust are explored in a fun and unobtrusive manner for the participants.

In traditional teaching models the teacher passed the knowledge onto the students. The students absorbed the information and learned it. In modern day teaching methods the learning approach is much more interactive. This interactive method is used in the Magic Workshop. The participants learn by doing, thus cultivating their own skills, with help from the facilitator where necessary. They in turn relay this information in the same format to other participants.

This shared-learning concept is hereby developed through regrouping the participants.

- Firstly, you need to gain the attention of every participant. Ask everybody to remain seated and to listen carefully.
- Go to each group and count off the members as shown below.

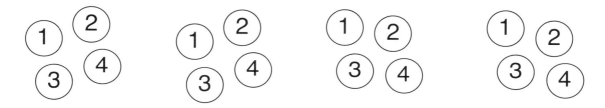

- Now, invite all the **ones** to stand up, holding their tricks, then direct these participants to one corner of the hall.
- Next, invite all the **twos** to stand up, holding their tricks and direct these to another corner of the hall.
- Repeat this procedure with the **threes**, then the **fours**.

In this way each new group will have four people with different tricks. Each member will meet and work with new people and while showing and teaching their tricks become the focus of attention for a short period in this new group.

Does it matter if you have an odd number of participants? Not at all! It doesn't make much difference what number you have. Just put the extra member or members into any groups. Two members showing the same trick can help each other and share the attention.

Performing their tricks

5

Performing a trick
Opportunity is provided for each person to perform their trick.

Now is the time in the Magic Workshop when communication and confidence building really begins. It occurs very naturally as a result of the participants trying to get an interesting message (trick) across in a fun way.

- Inform the groups that each person must get a chance to perform their trick for the other members of their new group. Explain to them that it is necessary for the other members to give their full attention to the performer at the time and to make sure that each person is treated equally.

- Now let them get on with it. The groups once again become very actively involved in the performing of their tricks and it is important to give them ample time to accomplish this task.
- You will need to move around briskly to each group to keep an eye out for any member who needs assistance in any way or to pep up any dull spots, which may occur within the groups during this process.

Teaching each other new tricks

6

Teaching each other new tricks
The participants share with each other the secret of their trick and how to perform it.

During the period of performing their tricks, the members should also explain to the other members of their new group how the trick is done and teach them how to do it.

Again, you will need to visit each group to keep reminding them of this and to ensure that every member understands each trick. Teaching each other how to do the trick strengthens their ability to do the trick properly. After all, one of the best ways to learn something is to try to teach it to somebody else! Being both student and teacher within a small group situation can be very beneficial to the participants. Such situations cultivate the development of listening and attentive skills whilst also promoting self-confidence and communication abilities.

Large group activity

7

Large group activity
Entertainment and fun for the
entire group
OR a group game
OR Make and Do.

Before distributing the magic packs, I usually get the whole group seated together and perform some magic for them. This adds another dimension and credibility to the whole Magic Workshop experience. If this is not possible then you could once more let them see you properly perform all the workshop tricks and puzzles as a kind of recapitulation period.

For the longer workshop, a Make and Do session where you perform a trick and have everyone make it up afterwards is an ideal addition to the workshop. The Make and Do section beginning on page 95 has some suitable tricks to use here.

A quick group game is also a nice way to bring the whole group together. My other book *Golden Hours: Games for Groups* has a large number of group games suitable for the longer workshop.

Distribution of give-away packs

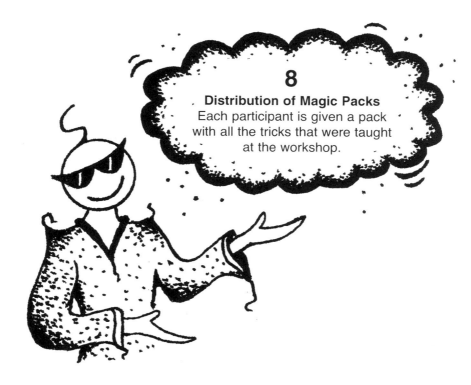

8
Distribution of Magic Packs
Each participant is given a pack with all the tricks that were taught at the workshop.

The Magic Workshop Give-away Packs should not be distributed until the end of the workshop as the participants will be so interested in the contents of the pack that it may prove quite difficult to gain their full attention afterwards. The whole affair needs to be carried out in an organised manner so a few ground rules are necessary.

- Before you distribute the packs request everyone to sit down.
- Once all are seated display the Give-away booklet-pack. Tell them that each person who remains seated will receive one of these.
- Go through the booklet-pack and explain briefly what they need to do to make up the tricks and puzzles contained therein.
- Now distribute one booklet-pack to each member.

Ending the workshop

It's important to end the workshop in a professional manner. Having distributed the Magic Packs, request the attention of the whole group. When everybody is listening give your end-of-workshop 'Thank You' speech.

- Thank the **organisers and the leaders** for hosting your Magic Workshop. Thank them too for their help with the workshop duties.
- Thank the **participants** for their attention and co-operation during the workshop.

Then, gather together all your workshop materials and remember to leave the room as you found it.

Part 2

Resources

Warm-up Activities

A warm-up game prepares the participants for the workshop by getting them directly involved as quickly as possible. Any self-consciousness that may exist quickly evaporates once the activity is under way and a more relaxed atmosphere follows.

This section contains three games that involve a lot of movement, interaction and fun. Each finishes with the group divided into smaller groups in readiness for the next stage of the programme. They are ideal for the Magic Workshop and any one should get you off to a strong start.

- The **Swap-around Game** was developed through numerous workshops to suit my requirements for the Magic Workshop. It is a very flexible game and can be lengthened or shortened to suit varying workshop needs.
- **Magic Mix** is a great game to liven up a group of participants. It also helps to promote concentration, awareness and observational skills and gets a workshop off to a great start.
- **Colour Dot Grouping** is a quiet, enjoyable game that demands silent co-operation and interaction from each individual player and easily divides the group into smaller groups.

The Swap-around Game

For a long time I searched for a suitable game that could be used as a warm-up activity and one that related favourably to the concept of the Magic Workshop. I didn't find any such game, although admittedly I was hard to please, so the Swap-around Game was invented. This game is the result of much fine-tuning in scores of workshops. It uses cards with trick pictures that change when turned upside-down. This gives the game a magical theme and introduces the mood of the workshop. It is a perfect warm-up activity; it has mystery, movement, music, anticipation, interaction, excitement, fun and a little gift for each player at the end. Use it in its entirety or chop and change it to suit the type of group you are working with.

Preparation

- Begin by photocopying pages 33, 34, 35, and 36. Use a different colour card for each page. Each page has four copies of the same trick-card so one copy of each page should give you enough cards for one workshop.
- You will also need some small envelopes.
- Cut out the trick-cards and put each one into a separate envelope. You will need one of these envelopes for each participant. Use small colour stickers to keep the envelopes closed. The colour of this sticker should match the colour of the trick-card inside.
- It's a good idea to make up a few extra ones in case there are extra participants on the day.

Procedure

- Mix up the envelopes and, with a marker, number the envelopes 1, 2, 3 etc. respective of the number of participants in the workshop.
- Give one envelope to each participant instructing them to keep the envelopes closed at this stage.

- Inform the players that you will now play some music during which they are to continuously exchange envelopes with other players and when the music stops they must freeze. Do not give any other instruction at this stage.
- Start the music (players exchange envelopes).
- Stop the music (players freeze). Make a big deal of watching the 'frozen' players and checking for any tiny signs of movement. Some will inevitably get a fit of the giggles here.
- Tell them that you will try that one more time and see if they can keep absolutely still. Start the music again.
- Stop the music (players freeze again). Check for movement. The players will react brilliantly and you have complete silence for the next instruction.
- Instruct the players to line up in numerical order as fast as they can and without talking.
- When they have completed this task congratulate them, and then ask whether or not they think they can do it faster next time.
- Start the music again (players exchange envelopes this time while walking backwards).
- Stop the music (players freeze). Direct them to line up in numerical order again. The players are usually faster at lining up the second time.
- Repeat this musical cards exchange twice more with the following commands when the music stops:
  - *Group together in colours (stickers on envelopes determine colours).*
  - *Group together so that in each group there is only one of each colour.*
- While grouped in this formation instruct the players to now open their envelopes, look at their trick-cards and look at other members' trick-cards also. Inform them that they may keep these cards.
- Keep this group formation for the next part of the workshop – the Group Focusing activity.

Note
The above game is ideal for the Magic Workshop warm-up stage and was developed with this purpose in mind. However, if you wish to use different warm-up activities this section details two other suitable games.

The Swap-around Game

Copy this page onto RED card.
Then cut out the individual cards and put each one into a separate envelope.

The Swap-around Game

Copy this page onto GREEN card.

Then cut out the individual cards and put each one into a separate envelope.

The Swap-around Game

Copy this page onto YELLOW card.
Then cut out the individual cards and put each one into a separate envelope.

The Swap-around Game

TO SEE WHAT THE GIRL SAW
AT THE CIRCUS TURN THE
CARD UPSIDE-DOWN

TO SEE WHAT THE GIRL SAW
AT THE CIRCUS TURN THE
CARD UPSIDE-DOWN

TO SEE WHAT THE GIRL SAW
AT THE CIRCUS TURN THE
CARD UPSIDE-DOWN

TO SEE WHAT THE GIRL SAW
AT THE CIRCUS TURN THE
CARD UPSIDE-DOWN

Copy this page onto BLUE card.
Then cut out the individual cards and put each one into a separate envelope.

Magic Mix

This is an excellent warm-up and group-mixing game. It also helps to develop awareness and observation skills. It is suitable for the Magic Workshop because it gets the players moving in a fun way and helps you to divide the group into teams in readiness for the next stage of the programme. You will, ideally, need twelve or more participants for this game.

The set up is to organise the group into a circle formation where each player, except one, is seated on a chair. The player without a chair stands in the centre of the circle. As the group leader, you should stand in the centre for the beginning of the game.

Procedure

- Standing in the centre, give each player one of the following magical item names: **rabbit**, **hat** or **wand**. Continue repeating these three items around the circle, so that there are, at least, three or four people with the same item name.

- Explain to the group that when you call out an item name (e.g. hats), all the players with that item name must swap places. The centre person (you, in this instance) must also try to get a chair during this swapping process. Whoever is left standing without a chair becomes the new centre person and continues the game by calling out another one of the magical item names.
- At any time, the centre person may call out **magic mix**. This means that every player must move and change places.
- Stop the game when you feel that it's the right time. Ask the group to team together in their magic item names (all 'rabbits' together, all 'hats' together and all 'wands' together).
- Keep this group formation for the next part of the workshop – the Group Focusing activity.

Notes

- Players rushing back and forth through the centre of the circle could crash against each other. Stress the need for careful and considerate movement.
- Sometimes, players have a tendency to jump over-enthusiastically into the chairs. Both the chair and the player can fall helplessly backwards. It is important to point out this danger before the game begins.

Colour Dot Grouping

This is a lovely quiet game to use as a warm-up and group-forming exercise. It gets the group helping each other at a very early stage and finishes with the participants formed into smaller groups.

You will need a packet of self-adhesive colour labels. If you can't obtain the colours, you can easily make your own by getting white labels and colouring them with markers. You won't need too many, so this shouldn't be much of a chore. Another alternative is to use colour plastic clothes pegs.

Procedure
- Have the players stand in a circle formation.
- Go around to the participants and stick a label or clothes peg onto the back of their tops. Make sure that they do not catch a glimpse of the colours on their backs. Arrange it so that, at least, three members get red, three get blue etc.
- On a signal from you, each participant must walk around the hall and help others to find their team colours. However, this help can only be given in the form of gestures – no talking is allowed at this stage. The objective is to get each colour grouped together.
- Eventually all the participants will be grouped together in small groups related to the colour on their backs.
- Keep this small group formation for the next stage of the workshop – the Group Focusing activity.

Group Focusing Activities

The four puzzles detailed in this section are perfect to use as group focusing activities within a magic workshop context. Ideal puzzles should be challenging but not seemingly impossible. You don't want the participants to become frustrated and give up too easily so the puzzle must look achievable. These puzzles are suitable for most groups.

- The step-by-step nature of **The Square Puzzle** and **The Triangle Puzzle** enables them to be presented to almost any age group.
- The fact that **The Horse and Rider Puzzle** has only got three picture pieces screams an *'I must be able to solve this!'* attitude in the minds of the participants.
- **The Word Puzzles Sheet** has enough variety to capture the imagination of any group for an extended period of time.

Remember to inform them that the Group Focusing Activity is a co-operation exercise and that they should work together as a team to find the solution.

The Square Puzzle

I really love this puzzle and you'll see why if you use it with your groups. It's a puzzle that can be presented to all age groups as it has several different levels. Because of its step-by-step nature it can be used to tease, bit by bit a young or older age group. When they have solved one level of it, you hit them with the next level and so on. There's nothing like a little success to encourage further participation and effort.

Preparation

- Make copies of The Square Puzzle on page 45. Card is better than paper for this. Use a different colour card for each copy. This will save you a lot of trouble during the workshop, as you will know that each colour makes up a complete square.
- Cut along the lines to make the six puzzle pieces. One complete square is required for each small group.

Procedure

- Begin by distributing pieces 1 and 2 to each group. Inform the groups that their task is to make a square from these two triangles and to tell you when they have succeeded in doing so. This stage is easy and all groups will think that it is too simple. However, this is an excellent way to begin the exercise. If the first stage is easy, the players will develop a confidence in their problem solving ability as a group. It starts the exercise on a successful note and the constant adding on of extra pieces develops a lively momentum.
- As the groups inform you of their success in solving a stage, give them the extra pieces to take them to the next level of the exercise.

The Square Puzzle can be taken to any of four levels and each stage is a complete puzzle in itself. The level at which you stop depends very much on the age and ability of the group you are working with. As a leader you can congratulate the groups on solving the puzzle at any of the levels and need not mention that a higher level exists. However some groups will require the higher level and this puzzle will certainly meet that challenge.

The Square Puzzle

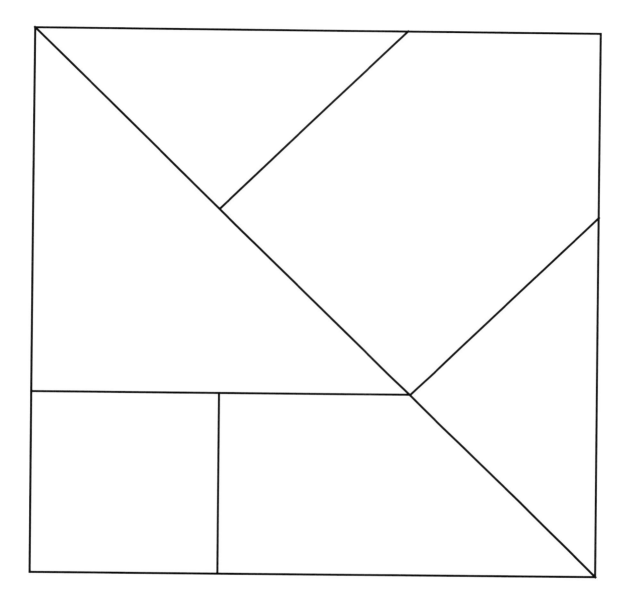

Copy this page onto strong card.
Then carefully cut out the six puzzle pieces.

The Square Puzzle

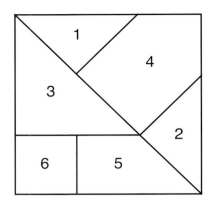

Challenge

Level 1
Make a square from pieces 1 and 2 ⟶

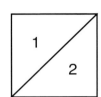

Level 2
Make a square from pieces 1, 2 and 3 ⟶

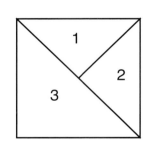

Level 3
Make a square from pieces 1, 2, 3, 4 and 5 ⟶

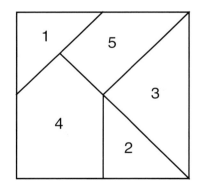

Level 4
Make a square from pieces 1, 2, 3, 4, 5 and 6 ⟶

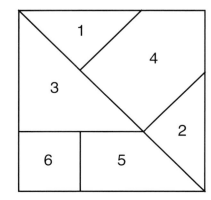

Solution

The Square Puzzle

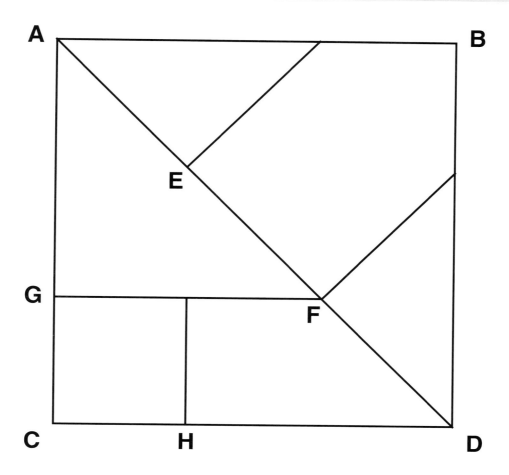

If you do not wish to use the photocopied version of **The Square Puzzle** here are the mathematical instructions for making up the puzzle yourself.

- Begin by drawing a square.
- Next draw the diagonal line AD.
- Trisect this diagonal line making three equal segments AE, EF and FD.
- Then draw a perpendicular line from E to meet the edge AB and a perpendicular line from F to meet the edge BD.
- From F draw a line parallel to CD meeting the edge AC at G.
- Now draw a perpendicular line from GF to meet the edge CD at H with respect to CH equalling the length GC.
- Cut out these six pieces and you've completed the making of The Square Puzzle.

The Triangle Puzzle

Like the Square Puzzle on the previous pages, the Triangle Puzzle also has several different levels. Each level requires that a triangle be produced from the supplied pieces. When a level has been solved, extra pieces are added to make the puzzle more challenging. The interesting aspect of this puzzle is that each higher level actually builds on the knowledge gained from the previous levels. I developed this puzzle myself using a tee-square and a 45-degree angle set-square but I'm sure that mathematicians out there will tell me that it is already documented elsewhere.

Preparation

- Make copies of The Triangle Puzzle on page 49. Card is better than paper for this. Use a different colour card for each copy of the triangle. This will save you a lot of trouble during the workshop when different pieces are liable to get mixed up. Trust me, this happens very easily!
- Cut along the lines to make the six puzzle pieces. One complete triangle is required for each small group.

Procedure

- Begin by distributing pieces 1 and 2 to each group. Inform the groups that their task is to make a triangle from these two pieces and to tell you when they have succeeded in doing so. This stage can be surprisingly tricky but all groups will get it rather quickly. As with the Square Puzzle, the constant adding on of extra pieces develops a lively momentum.
- As the groups inform you of their success in solving a stage, give them the extra pieces to take them to the next level of the exercise.

The Triangle Puzzle can be stopped at any level depending on the age and ability of the group you are working with. Older groups will require the tougher challenges and the Triangle Puzzle has enough pieces to meet these demands.

The Triangle Puzzle

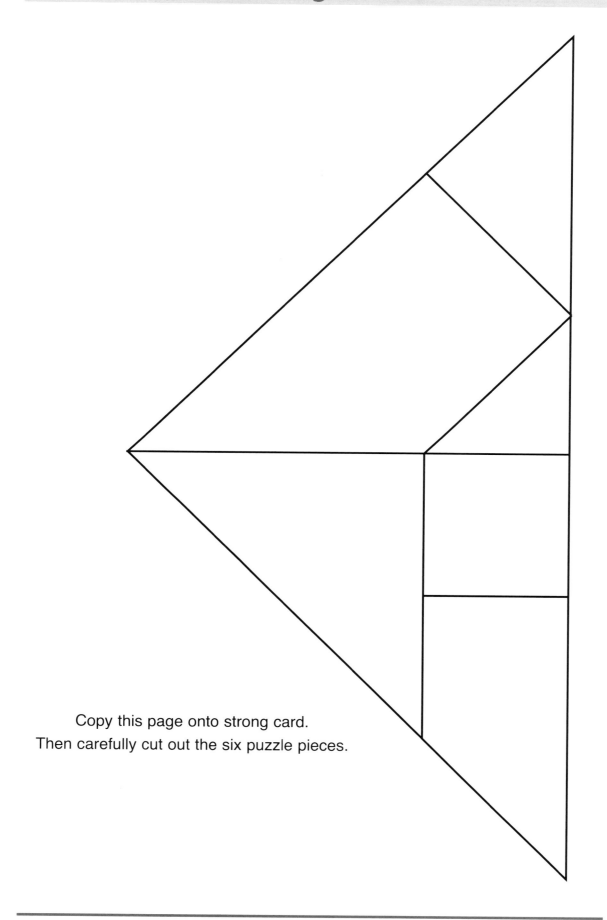

Copy this page onto strong card.
Then carefully cut out the six puzzle pieces.

The Triangle Puzzle

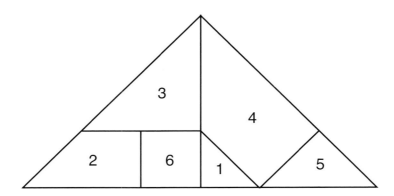

Challenge	Solution

Level 1
Make a triangle from pieces 1 and 2 ⟶

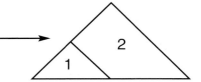

Level 2
Make a triangle from pieces 1, 2 and 3 ⟶

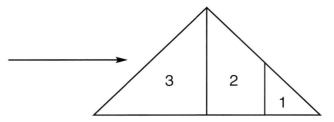

Level 3
Make a triangle from pieces
1, 2, 3, 4 and 5 ⟶

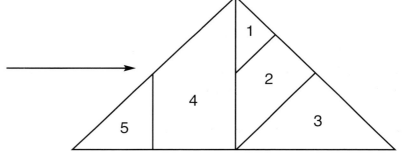

Level 4
Make a triangle from pieces
1, 2, 3, 4, 5 and 6 ⟶

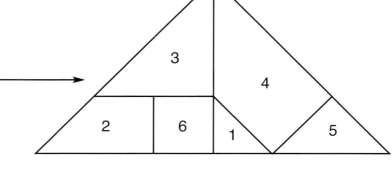

The Triangle Puzzle

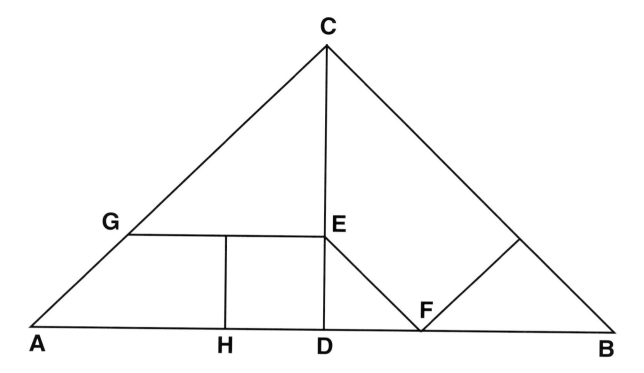

If you do not wish to use the photocopied version of **The Triangle Puzzle** here are the mathematical instructions for making up the puzzle yourself.

- Begin by drawing the base line AB.
- Then from A and B, draw 45-degree lines to meet at point C (creating a right angle).
- Drop a line from C perpendicular to and meeting AB at D.
- Calculate one third of CD to find point E.
- Draw a 45-degree line from E to meet DB at F.
- From F draw a 45-degree line to meet the edge CB.
- Then from E draw a line parallel to AD to meet the edge AC at G.
- Now drop a perpendicular line from GE to meet AD at H so that HD equals the length of ED.
- Finally cut out the six pieces and you have completed the making of the Triangle Puzzle.

The Horse and Rider Puzzle

This is a very clever puzzle. It consists of just three cards – two showing pictures of horses and a third which depicts the two riders, one of which is upside-down.

The problem is to put the cards together in such a way that the completed picture shows the two riders on the horses in their proper riding positions. Bending, cutting or folding the cards is not allowed.

A three-piece jigsaw sounds easy, doesn't it? But give this one a try without looking at the solution and you'll see why it's so clever. I don't know who first invented this puzzle as various versions of it have appeared in different puzzle books over the years. It's a fantastic attention grabber and an excellent group initiative. Watch them scratch their heads over this one!

The version provided here is one that I drew up myself and is styled on the logo for my own magic workshop.

Preparation

- Make copies of The Horse and Rider Puzzle on page 53. Card is better than paper for this.
- Cut around the boxes to make a set of three cards. One set is required for each small group.

Procedure

- Distribute one three-piece puzzle set to each team.
- Inform the teams that their task is to put the cards together in such a way that the completed picture shows the two riders on the horses in their proper riding positions.
- Make sure to tell them that bending, cutting or folding the cards is not allowed.

The Horse and Rider Puzzle

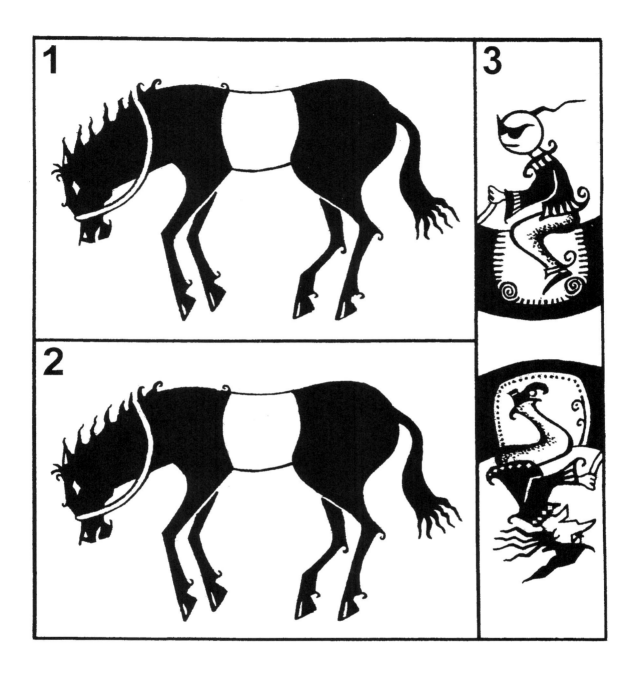

Copy this page onto strong card.
Then carefully cut out the three cards.

The Horse and Rider Puzzle

Place card 1 and card 2 together so that the two horses are back to back.

Then place card 3 across the two cards to make two horses and riders, one of which is upside-down.

The Word Puzzles Sheet

These word puzzles are a definite favourite with most groups. Participants seem to enjoy working together to brainstorm the hidden meanings.

Each picture box represents a well-known word or phrase. For example:

B G **O** E **T** N **T** I L **E** **E** = a genie in a bottle

It's important to have a mix of difficult and easy ones so that a group can appreciate both challenge and success.

You'll think of other ones yourself but be careful – they're addictive!

Preparation
- Make copies of page 56. You will need one copy for each small group.
- You will also need to pack pens or pencils for each group.

Procedure
- Distribute a copy of Word Puzzles to each group.
- Inform them that their objective is to work together in their groups to solve as many of the word puzzles as they can and to write their answers in the spaces provided.

The Word Puzzles Sheet

Y R R U H ①	WHEATHER ②	.THAT'S ③	ONCE ――― A TIME ④
X Q Q Q M E ⑤	STAND ――― I ⑥	S S I I D D E E ⑦	VAD ERS ⑧
GET IT GET IT GET IT GET IT ⑨	PRO/MISE ⑩	ABCDEF GHIJKL MNOPQR STVW XYZ ⑪	MILONELION ⑫
CYCLE CYCLE CYCLE ⑬	ECNALG ⑭	LU CKY ⑮	You JUST me ⑯
LAL ⑰	AID← AID AID ⑱	.....ii ⑲	JACK ⑳

1. _____
2. _____
3. _____
4. _____
5. _____
6. _____
7. _____
8. _____
9. _____
10. _____

11. _____
12. _____
13. _____
14. _____
15. _____
16. _____
17. _____
18. _____
19. _____
20. _____

The Word Puzzles Sheet

Answers

1. Hurry up

2. A bad spell of weather

3. That's beside the point

4. Once upon a time

5. Excuse me

6. I understand

7. Side by side

8. Space invaders

9. Forget it

10. Broken promise

11. Missing you

12. One in a million

13. Tricycle

14. Glance backwards

15. Lucky break

16. Just between you and me

17. All mixed up

18. First aid

19. Spots before the eyes

20. Jack in the box

Concerns with Revelations – A Note to Magicians

As a magician, I am well aware of the concern that exists among magicians and magic organisations regarding the unnecessary exposure of magical secrets to the general public. I respect this concern and indeed support the excellent work that the world's magic organisations do pertaining to this aspect of our art. Without this respect for its secrets, magic would lose a very essential ingredient and would cease to be magic in the eyes of the audience. Magic is a form of entertainment made possible by its secrets and therefore these should quite rightly, and necessarily, be protected with respect and regard for all magicians. However, this respect should embody all levels of genuinely interested practitioners, including beginners and their rights to learn the art.

I believe that the worst form of exposure is that which results from bad presentation. Of course, the solution to this problem is practice, practice and more practice. All magicians whether amateur or professional have a special magical duty to protect and uphold the secrets of our art. This book is produced with the utmost respect for the art of magic and as such I know it does not neglect this duty.

Many of the tricks used in the Magic Workshop are puzzle or mathematically based. They were especially chosen or developed to suit the Magic Workshop situation. Their secrets, if you could call them secrets, are not exposed for the sake of exposure and are certainly no threat to the acts of professional magicians. In fact, far from being a threat I have found that they create interest and a healthy respect for the art of magic and magicians and this is something which should be nurtured for the benefit of the future of magic as a performing art.

At the end of my workshops, I perform a short magic show using tricks from my own repertoire. There is never any question of exposure at this stage – it is simply a magic show and is the easiest magic show for kids that a magician could ever do. The interest created by the magic in the Magic Workshop is clearly obvious and they watch with great enthusiasm.

Yes, we need to be vigilant concerning the protection of the secrets but we also need to create little avenues of openness for the future generations of magicians. After all, isn't that how most of us became interested in the art!

About the Tricks

These tricks have been specially chosen and produced for the Magic Workshop. A considerable amount of thought, work, trial and error has gone into their selection to ensure their suitability for this type of workshop situation. Many other tricks tried and tested over the years just didn't fit the requirements for one reason or another. The following criteria are used when working on the production of these effects:

The tricks must be:

- Easy to make
- Cost effective
- Pack flat
- Easy to teach
- Easy to perform

Easy to make

An important feature of the workshop is the give-away aspect of the tricks. I was running more and more workshops so I had to find an easy way to produce the tricks without sacrificing the all-important ingredient of quality. I didn't want to use cheap plastic commercial props, or to expose professional magic secrets. As time was an important factor, each trick, together with its instructions, was produced on a single piece of card. These are also easy to customise and look attractive and professional. The participants receive them in booklet form at the end of the workshop. It is an easy matter for them to cut out the props when they get home. I redesigned, or in many cases invented, tricks to suit my own requirements. Also, my name appears on every item in my magic pack booklet. Contact numbers and workshop details are included in each pack and also appear on the cover.

Cost effective

All the materials required for the magic workshop are cheap and easy to obtain. I realize that funds are tight with most clubs, and every business looks for ways to keep costs at a minimum. I don't see the point in squandering funds on commercially available items that turn out to be unsuitable workshop material. This book is all-inclusive and anyone using it can reproduce these tricks cheaply and easily.

Pack flat

As all working professionals know, ideal items are ones that pack flat and play big. Valuable space is not wasted in storage and great effect is achieved in presentation. Every item in the Magic Workshop fits into the pack-flat category. Even such things as stacking plastic cups take up very little room in the bag. This is a very important feature for the workshop facilitator.

Easy to teach

Even easy magic tricks are hard to teach and many require a certain level of skill that cannot successfully be acquired by a participant in a short workshop situation.

Therefore, tricks that require tricky handling to pull off the magic effect are definitely out. The tricks and their methods must be easy to communicate to the participant. Tricks that work because of the way a card is turned or folded and mathematically based tricks are ideal. Remember that the participant is not a student of magic. You are not teaching magic. You are facilitating a fun, confidence inspiring, communication-type workshop; therefore the methods must be easy to convey to each participant.

Easy to perform

Magic is a skill. It is an art form that takes many years of practice. Sleight of hand takes countless hours of solitary work and determination. That is why the tricks in the magic workshop are of a particular calibre. Success in handling the trick must be almost instant for the participant or you will lose a very important ingredient of the magic workshop concept – namely 'participant confidence'. This isn't the time for clever moves or complicated routines. The magic trick used here is the vehicle for an experiential learning process, all of which happens during the workshop and reciprocates long afterwards through its positive effects.

Components of each trick

Each trick will be dealt with separately and formatted the same way:

Skill level	Tricks are rated on a scale of **Level 1** to **Level 3**. None of the tricks are particularly difficult but you'll notice that **Level 1** tricks are almost self-working while **Level 2** and **Level 3** demand a little more concentration.
Production	What to do to get the trick ready for the workshop.
Effect	How the trick looks from a spectator's point of view.
How it works	Explains the means by which the illusion is accomplished.
Presentation	How you, as a leader, should present the trick to the groups.

Choose the tricks you wish to use with your group. You will need about four or five tricks during the workshop.

Three Pieces

Skill level 1

Production

All you need for this trick are a few pieces of paper. Any printer should have a batch of off-cuts to keep you going for dozens of workshops. About ten pieces for each member of a small group is enough for their practice and performances.

Effect

A piece of paper, torn almost into thirds is displayed and a spectator is challenged to tear the paper into three pieces in one go while holding the paper as illustrated and pulling the hands apart.

It looks easy but proves to be an impossible task. However you show that it can be accomplished.

How it works

Trying to tear a piece of paper as described above is really an impossible stunt. It can't be done. No matter how many times you try it, one piece will always tear off leaving the other two pieces together.

However, you (clever person that you are) can accomplish this task by grasping the centre segment of the paper between your teeth and tearing away the outer segments.

Cheating? Maybe, but the challenge was to tear the paper into three pieces in one go while holding the paper as described and that is what you do!

Presentation

- Approach the small group with the batch of papers and tear one piece almost into thirds in preparation for the challenge.
- Challenge the group members to tear the paper into three pieces in one go, by pulling the hands apart and while holding an end piece in each hand.
- When each member of the group has tried and failed, explain that with a little honest cheating it can be done. Explain the method by which this can be accomplished.
- Now ask them to practice the wording of the challenge: 'I challenge you to tear this paper into three pieces in one go, while holding an end piece in each hand.'
- Give a number of papers to each member of this group and invite them to spend some time testing out the workings of this challenge.
- Tell them that they will shortly get a chance to present the trick to the other groups.
- Allow them some time to practice the trick.

The Magic Wands

Skill level 1

Production

Using good quality card, photocopy page 67 and then cut out the two cards carefully. You will need a set of cards for each member of a small group.

Effect

You put a two-piece jigsaw together to show a picture of five magic wands. Then just by moving the cards apart and bringing them together again, you cause one of the wands to disappear.

How it works

The nice thing about this trick is that even when you know how it works it still fascinates. The secret lies in the way the wands have been drawn on the two cards. When the cards are separated and brought back together again, the lower card is moved a little to the right. This causes a wand to apparently disappear.

Presentation

- Approach the small group and display the two cards together depicting five magic wands.

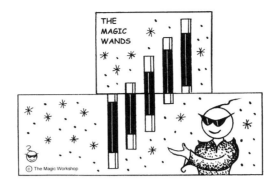

- Draw attention to the fact that there are FIVE magic wands in the picture.
- Separate the two cards. Click your fingers or make some other magical gesture.

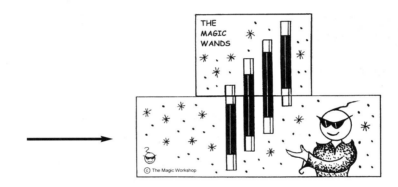

- Now bring the cards back together again, making sure to slide the bottom card to the right to match up the four bottom wands with the four top wands.
- A strange thing has happened. One of the wands has disappeared.
- Explain the simple working of the trick.
- Now tell the group members that they must spend some time getting accustomed to the handling of the trick because they will shortly get a chance to present it to the other groups.
- Give a set of cards to each member of this group.
- Allow them some time to practice the trick.

The Magic Wands

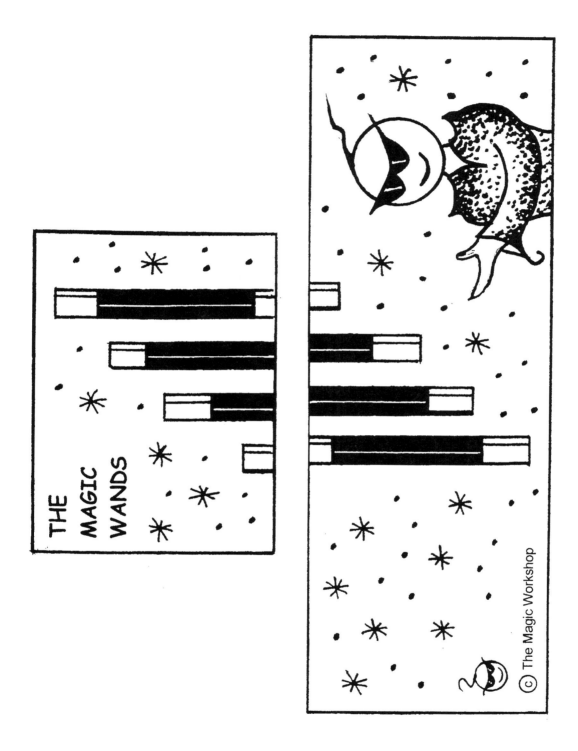

Copy this page onto strong card.

Then cut out the two cards.

Girl and Dog

Skill level 1

Production

Using good quality card, photocopy the card on page 70 and then cut it out carefully. You will need one of these cards for each member in a small group.

Effect

A card with a picture of a girl is shown. The card is turned around showing the back. When the front is shown again the girl has turned into a dog.

How it works

The picture is a two-way drawing. It portrays a girl when viewed one way and when viewed upside-down depicts a dog.

Presentation

- Approach the group and exhibit the card as a girl.
- Hold the card in both hands with the girl-picture facing your audience.
- Tell them to watch carefully as you turn the card bottom-over-top as shown below.

- Then turn the card side-over-side as shown below.

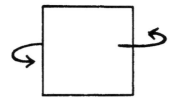

- This action turns the picture upside down in an imperceptible manner and the resulting picture change is quite magical, especially to younger workshop participants.
- Now explain the moves of the trick to the group.
- Tell the members that they should now spend the next few minutes practising the trick because they will shortly get a chance to present it to the other groups.
- Give a card to each member of this group.
- Allow them some time to practice the trick but call back to check their progress.

Girl and Dog

Copy this page onto strong card.
Then cut out the picture card.

The Magnetic Spiral

Skill level 2

Production

Using good quality card, photocopy the spiral card on page 73 and then cut it out carefully. You will need one card for each member of a small group.

Effect

You exhibit the spiral card and explain that it has strange magnetic properties. To prove your claim you cause a person's hand to stick to their head with the aid of the card.

How it works

Of course the spiral card does not have any magnetic qualities. The secret lies in the fact that it is almost impossible to remove the hand by exerting pressure on the wrist through an upward movement. This upward movement, coupled with the fact that the wrist and arm are attached to the shoulder, puts the second person at a total disadvantage.

Presentation

- Approach the group and exhibit the spiral card.
- Tell the group that the spiral has magnetic qualities. Rub it on your sleeve to focus the magnetic energy (use your acting skills here) surrounding the spiral.
- Now place the spiral on a member's head and get them to place their hand against the card as shown in the illustration below. Explain that they must press hard against the card.

- Next invite another person to grasp the cardholder's wrist and try to lift the hand from the card without jerking.
- If the cardholder applies firm pressure on the card, the second person will find it very difficult to move the hand away from the card.
- Now inform them that, of course, the spiral is really not magnetic but that this explanation helps to distract the audience from the real secret which is as explained above.
- Explain to them that they must now practice the trick with each other and also be able to spin the yarn that the spiral card is magnetic. Tell them that they will shortly get a chance to present the trick to the other groups.
- Give a spiral card to each member of this group.
- Allow them some time to practice the trick.

The Magnetic Spiral

Copy this page onto strong card.
Then cut out the spiral card.

Finger Freezer

Skill level 2

Production

Using good quality card, photocopy the Snowflake Card on page 75 and then cut it out carefully. You will need one card for each member in a small group.

Effect

You display a picture of a snowflake with which you proceed to render someone's finger strangely immobile.

How it works

Of course you don't really freeze the finger (as if you didn't know!). This trick works because of the natural muscular tension created by folding the middle finger, which in turn renders the ring finger immobile.

Presentation

- Approach the group and ask one person to place a hand on the floor and to fold the middle finger as shown below.
- Now display the snowflake card and explain that it has the power to freeze one of their fingers.
- Place the snowflake card underneath their ring finger and explain that this will cause the finger to become momentarily frozen.
- Invite the volunteer to try lifting all fingers, one at a time, but not the ring finger just yet. They will find this an easy task.
- Now ask them to try to lift the ring finger and watch as they struggle without success.
- Next explain the working of the trick to the group and have them practice for a little while. Tell them that they will shortly get a chance to show it to the other groups.
- Give a snowflake card to each member of this group.
- Allow them some time to practice the trick but call back to check their progress.

Finger Freezer

Copy this page onto strong card.
Then cut out the snowflake card.

Sneaky Snakes

Skill level 2

Production

Using good quality card, photocopy the three cards on page 78 and then cut them out carefully. You will need a set of cards for each member in a small group.

Effect

Three cards are placed side by side to make a picture of two long snakes. The cards are picked up and given a gentle shake. When put back down again, the snakes have changed in length.

How it works

This is really a three-piece jigsaw with an unusual middle section. Twisting this section around changes the lengths of the snakes.

Presentation

- Approach the group and display the three cards together to show two long snakes.
- Draw attention to the equal lengths of the two snakes.
- Turn all three cards over sideways in the direction indicated by the arrows.

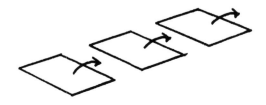

- The cards are now upside-down.
- Make some magical gesture over the cards, then turn the cards face upwards again as illustrated below. Note that the middle card is turned end-over-end instead of sideways, effectively twisting it 180 degrees.

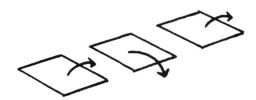

- Push the cards together to show that the snakes have changed in length.
- Turn the cards upside-down again saying 'And there's nothing on the back!' This action prevents the 'wise guys' getting too familiar with the design of the middle card.
- Now explain the secret of the trick to the group. Go through all the above moves with them.
- Tell the members that they should now spend the next few minutes practising the trick because they will shortly get a chance to present it to the other groups.
- Give a set of cards to each member of this group.
- Allow them some time to practice the trick but call back to check their progress.

Sneaky Snakes

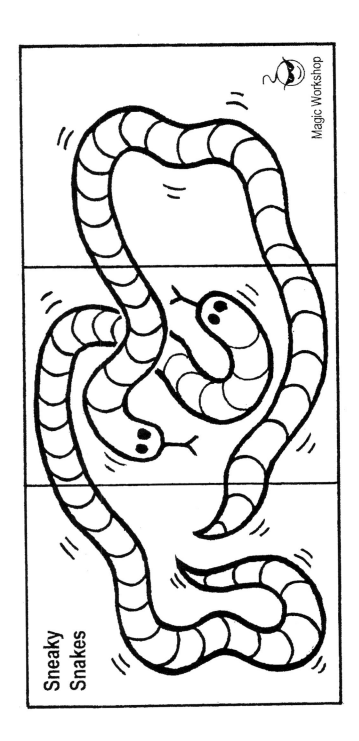

Copy this page onto strong card.
Then cut out the three cards.

The Linking Rings

Skill level 2

Production

Using good quality card, photocopy the three cards on page 81 and then cut them out carefully. You will need a set of cards for each member in a small group.

Effect

Three cards are placed side by side to make a picture of a magician with two sets of rings (one set linked, one set unlinked). The cards are picked up and given a gentle shake. When put back down again, the picture has changed. Rings that were **linked** are now **unlinked**, and vice versa.

How it works

This is really a three-piece jigsaw with an unusual middle section. Twisting this section around changes the picture.

Presentation

- Approach the group and display the three cards together to show a **linked** set on the left and an **unlinked** set on the right.
- Call attention to the linked and unlinked nature of the two sets of rings.

- Turn all three cards over sideways in the direction indicated by the arrows.

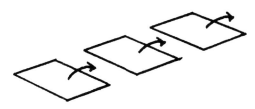

- The cards are now upside-down.
- Make some magical gesture over the cards, then turn the cards face upwards again as illustrated below. Note that the middle card is turned end-over-end instead of sideways, effectively twisting it 180 degrees.

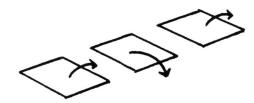

- Push the cards together to show that the linked rings have become unlinked and the unlinked set have become linked.
- Turn the cards upside-down again saying 'And there's nothing on the back!' This action prevents the 'wise guys' getting too familiar with the design of the middle card.
- Now explain the secret of the trick to the group. Go through all the above moves with them.
- Tell the members that they should now spend the next few minutes practising the trick because they will shortly get a chance to present it to the other groups.
- Give a set of cards to each member of this group.
- Allow them some time to practice the trick but call back to check their progress.

The Linking Rings

Copy this page onto strong card.
Then cut out the three cards.

Peg the Picture Card

Skill level 2

Production

To make this trick you will need five playing cards, one of which should be a picture card, a two-inch bulldog clip and an ordinary spring clothes peg. Overlap the cards in a straight row with the picture card in the centre. Trap the cards within a bulldog clip as shown in the picture.

Effect

In a line of five cards it seems an easy task to find the one picture card. However, spectators will be amazed, as they are way off the mark each time.

How it works

This is a very clever optical illusion produced by the discrepancy between the ways in which cards overlap differently, when turned face-up and then face-down. To properly understand this illusion, you will need to make it up first.

Presentation

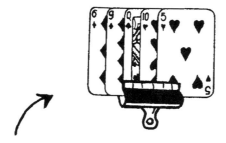

- Approach the group with the prearranged cards. Holding the cards face-up, stress the position of the picture card. Holding the bulldog clip, turn the cards over.

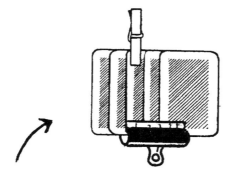

- Ask someone to mark the picture card by fastening a peg over its end

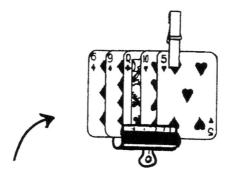

- Now turn the cards face-up again and, amazingly, the peg will not be on the picture card.
- Next explain to the group how the trick works.
- Give a pre-arranged card set to each member of this group and allow them time to become familiar with the overlapping arrangement of the cards
- Tell the members that they should now spend the next few minutes practising the trick because they will shortly get a chance to present it to the other teams.
- Allow them some time to practice the trick but call back to check their progress.

Magic Choice

Skill level 3

Production

Using good quality card, photocopy the two cards on page 86 and then cut them out carefully. You will need a set of cards for each member in a small group.

Effect

You show a card depicting six magical items. Someone randomly chooses one item and you prove that you already knew what their choice would be.

How it works

The secret to this effect is based on what magicians call a **force**. A force is a method of influencing a person's choice. The person believes that the choice is fair. The force employed here is a counting force used to arrive at the number **three** each and every time. The item at the third position is the **wand**; therefore **wand** will be the 'chosen' item.

Presentation

- Approach the group and place the prediction card face downwards. Tell the group that this is a prediction of something that is going to happen very shortly.
- Exhibit the Magic Choice card and call attention to the six different objects.

- Invite one person to pick a number between ONE and SIX. This choice is really quite free. When they tell you their chosen number you continue in the following manner:

If they pick ONE,	spell O,N,E, down from the top.
If they pick TWO,	spell T,W,O, down from the top.
If they pick THREE,	count 1,2,3, down from the top.
If they pick FOUR,	count 1,2,3,4, up from the bottom.
If they pick FIVE,	spell F,I,V,E, up from the bottom.
If they pick SIX,	spell S,I,X, down from the top.

  So you see, in this way, any number can bring them to 'choose' the **wand**. To prove that you knew they would 'choose' the **wand**, turn the prediction card face up to reveal the message 'You will choose the wand'.
- Now inform the group that you are going to explain how the trick is done and that they must practice it for a little while. Explain that they will shortly get a chance to show it to the other groups.
- Continue by explaining how the trick works as described above.
- Give a set of cards to each member of this group.
- Tell them that each person should do the trick for another in the group to help them become familiar with the method.
- Allow them some time to practice the trick but call back to check their progress.

Magic Choice

Copy this page onto strong card.
Then cut out the two cards.

Tricky Tumblers

Skill level 3

Production

For this trick you will need a set of three plastic tumblers for each member of a small group.

Effect

You do some movements with three tumblers that your audience is unable to duplicate successfully.

How it works

You make a subtle change to the starting line-up of the tumblers, effectively making it impossible for your audience to succeed.

Presentation

- Approach the group and place the three tumblers in front of them, middle tumbler mouth upwards and the other two mouth downwards as shown below.

- Demonstrate how with **three** moves only, you can finish with the three tumblers mouth upwards. Each move must consist of turning two tumblers at the same time, one in each hand.

    Move 1 – Turn tumblers 1 and 2
    Move 2 – Turn tumblers 1 and 3
    Move 3 – Turn tumblers 1 and 2 again.

  The three tumblers will now be mouths upwards as shown below.

- Challenge someone to do the same but before they begin, turn the centre tumbler mouth down. This now puts the tumblers in a different starting position as shown below:

  Now whichever way they attempt it, they will not end with all three tumblers mouth upwards. Even if they make the same moves as you demonstrated their cups will all be face downwards.

- Now explain the secret of the trick to the group. Go through all the above moves with them.
- Tell the members that they should now spend the next few minutes practising the trick because they will shortly get a chance to present it to the other groups.
- Give three tumblers to each member of this group.
- Allow them some time to practice the trick but call back to check their progress.

Lion to Girl

Skill level 3

Production

Using a light quality paper, photocopy the lion picture on page 91 and then cut it out carefully. Fold the picture as described below. You will need one of these pre-folded pictures for each member in a small group.

Effect

You display a piece of paper, which shows a picture of a lion. By folding the paper in a special way it shows the lion changing into a girl.

How it works

There is no secret to this effect. The audience knows what you are doing. You simply fold the picture in a special way and some of the lion's lines come together to form the girl.

Presentation

- Approach the group and display the (unfolded) lion picture. Then tell them to watch carefully and you will show them how to turn the lion into a girl.
- Fold the top half of the paper zigzag fashion as shown below.

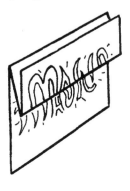

- Now fold the left side of the folded paper zigzag fashion as shown below. The girl appears.

- Give a pre-folded picture to each member of this group.
- Demonstrate the folding method to the group. Have them try it with their own pictures while you are with them.
- Tell the members that they will need to practice the folds, as they will shortly get a chance to present the trick to the other groups.
- Allow them some time to practice the trick but call back to check their progress.

Lion to Girl

Copy this page onto light quality paper.
Then cut out the picture.

Birthday Cards

Skill level 3

Production

Using good quality card, photocopy the number cards on page 94 and then cut them out carefully. You will need one set of cards for each member in a small group.

Effect

With five number cards you are mysteriously able to tell people when their birthday is.

How it works

You are able to tell the birthday by adding together the top left-hand-corner numbers on the chosen cards.

Presentation

- Approach the group and display the five number cards.
- Ask a member to think of their birthday and to indicate to you which card or cards contain this number.

2	10	18	26
3	11	19	27
6	14	22	30
7	15	23	31

8	12	24	28
9	13	25	29
10	14	26	30
11	15	27	31

= 10

- By silently adding together the top left-hand-corner numbers on these chosen cards, you are able to tell what their birthday is.
- Now explain the secret of the trick to the group.
- Tell the members that they should now spend the next few minutes practising the trick because they will shortly get a chance to present it to the other groups.
- Give a set of cards to each member of this group.
- Allow them some time to practice the trick but call back to check their progress.

Birthday Cards

1	9	17	25
3	11	19	27
5	13	21	29
7	15	23	31

8	12	24	28
9	13	25	29
10	14	26	30
11	15	27	31

2	10	18	26
3	11	19	27
6	14	22	30
7	15	23	31

16	20	24	28
17	21	25	29
18	22	26	30
19	23	27	31

4	12	20	28
5	13	21	29
6	14	22	30
7	15	23	31

Copy this page onto strong card.
Then cut out the five cards.

Make and do Tricks for the Longer Workshop

Another feature of the Magic Workshop is its potential for creativity. As well as the creativity that is occasioned by the participants during the learning, presenting and teaching stages, further opportunities for creativity can be produced by having a Make and Do section during the workshop. This is very stimulating and great fun for the participants. In this section, three such tricks are detailed:

- Begin by creating a working area in the corner. Protect the floor by spreading some newspapers on it. Set up the materials required. This should only take a couple of minutes at most.
- Next gather the group together and get them seated on the floor in another area of the hall.
- Now demonstrate the chosen trick to allow the members to see the effect from an audience's point of view.
- Afterwards explain how the trick works. Then take them through the steps to enable them to make it for themselves.
- Next distribute all the necessary materials to each member.
- They now set about making up the trick. You, and any other leaders present, should go around to all the members who may need assistance to make the trick properly. Also encourage the participants to help each other during this stage.
- When this 'make and do' stage is completed, have the participants help you to tidy up the workspace. Requesting nicely *'John, would you mind collecting the glue sticks, please?'* will always ensure a co-operative response.
- Once all this has been accomplished ask for volunteers to come to the front of the room to demonstrate the trick they have just made. This is a high focus time for such participants but many of them will relish the challenge and enjoy the fun of the whole experience.

The Magic Envelope

Making the trick

What you need
- Two identical envelopes
- Glue
- Two playing cards of the same value but different colour (e.g. ace of clubs and ace of hearts)

What you do
- Take the two envelopes and turn one upside-down.
- Put some glue on the address sides of the envelopes, then glue the two of them together as shown in the illustration. Make sure that there is no overlap.

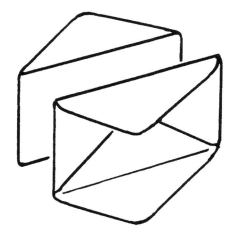

- The end result will look like one envelope with two flap sides.
- Put the red playing card inside the back envelope and close the flap. Now you are ready to perform.

Doing the trick
- Display the black playing card to your audience.
- Pick up the envelope, making sure that the spectators only see the front one.
- Tip it over so that they can see it is empty.
- Put the black card inside and close the flap.
- Place the envelope on a table, turning it over as you do so. Done casually this is never noticed. Now the back envelope is on top.
- Make some magical gestures, pick up the envelope and open it to show that the black card has changed into a red card.

Balancing a Tumbler on a Card

Making the trick

What you need
- Two playing cards
- Glue
- Tumbler

What you do
- Take one of the cards and fold it in half lengthways.
- Put some glue on one half.
- Paste this to the back of the second card.
- This makes a secret hinged flap, which when moved back with the thumb, will hold the tumbler upright.

Doing the trick
- To make it look like you are using an ordinary card begin by showing a deck of cards. The prepared card should be on top of the deck.
- Remove the prepared card and hold it in the left hand. Take the tumbler in the right hand and as you show it, secretly open the flap of the card.
- Very carefully, place the tumbler on the card. Of course you must pretend that it is very difficult and only leave the tumbler on the card for a very short time.
- Remove the tumbler with one hand while the other hand takes the card and secretly closes the flap.

The Jumping Spider

Making the trick

What you need
- Two small squares of paper about 100mm x 100mm
- Pencil

What you do
- On one of the sheets draw a picture of a spider. Be creative here. Make it scary.
- On the other sheet draw a large web.

Doing the trick
- Lay the spider picture diagonally on a table with one corner pointing towards you.

- Then place the web picture on top, covering the spider, but a little further away.

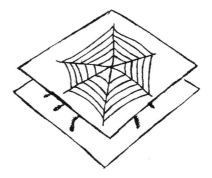

- Now using the pencil, start rolling them together from the corner nearest you.

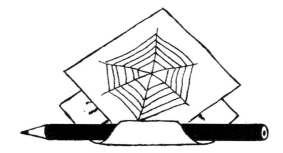

- When they are almost completely rolled up, the corner of the spider sheet will flip over the web sheet. Stop immediately when this happens.
- Unroll the sheets and you will find that the spider has jumped to the top.
- Scary!

The Give-away Magic Pack

The Magic Workshop Give-away Pack is an attractive and popular feature of the Magic Workshop. The participants love to have something to take home and the bookers are usually impressed. The Give-away pack is easy to make up and shouldn't take too long. Copy onto card rather than paper. I use two-sheet card. It is also nice to use as many different colours of card as you can. You will notice that the trick instructions are simplified in the Give-away pack version. Remember that the participants have practised the trick during the workshop so these instructions only serve to remind them of what they have already learned.

Making up the give-away magic pack

Procedure
- Make copies of the **Magic Pack** cover on page 104.
- Make copies of '**Certificate of Participation**' on page 106.
- Make copies of '**Tricks of the Trade**' on page 105.
- Make copies of the **puzzle** you intend to use in your Magic Workshop.
- Make copies of the **tricks** you intend to use in your Magic Workshop.
- Make copies of one or two of the '**Give-away**' items on pages 125-130.

- When these copies have been made, place all the sheets together in the following order:

  from the top down:
  - Cover
  - Certificate of Participation
  - Tricks of the Trade
  - Puzzle
  - Workshop Tricks
  - Give-away Items
- Now staple them at the sides or, for a more professional look, use slide binders.

You will need one of these packs for each participant in the workshop.

Magicians' tricks of the trade

When you do a trick, the effect is magical to someone
who doesn't know its secret.
Never tell anyone how a trick is done.

Spend some time practising so that you know
you can do the trick.
Don't expect to be able to do the trick immediately.
By practising the trick over and over again, the trick
becomes more magical in your hands.

Never do a trick more than once for the same people.
They will know what to expect the second time around, so it
will be easier for them to spot how the trick is done.

Three Pieces

Cut out the rectangular piece above or use any similar small pieces of paper. Tear it almost into thirds as shown below.

Ask someone to hold one of the end pieces in each hand and attempt to tear the paper into three pieces in one go.

It looks easy, but when they try it, only one piece tears off. The result will be the same no matter how many times they try.

However, the problem can be solved with a little cheating. Hold as above, then grasp the centre piece between your teeth as you tear away the outer pieces.

The Magic Wands

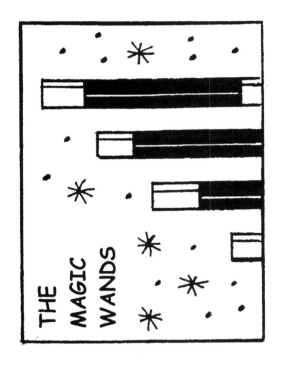

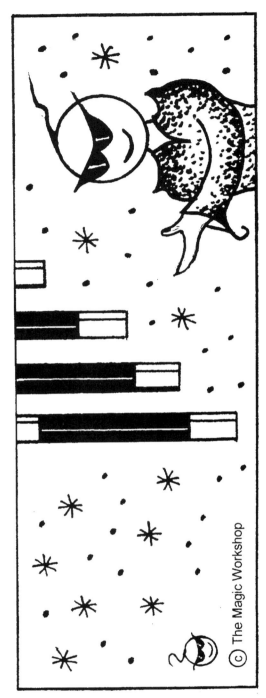

© The Magic Workshop

Cut out the two cards and place them together as shown here. Sliding one card to the left or right makes one of the wands appear or disappear.

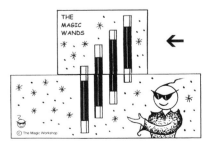

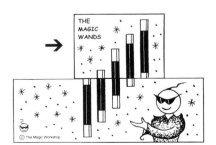

Girl and Dog

Cut out the picture above.

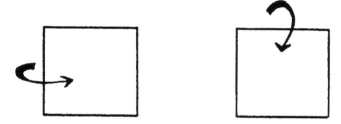

Hold the picture in both hands with the picture facing your audience.

Turn the picture around to face yourself. Now turn it around again, but this time, turn it upside-down also. This will show a changed picture to your audience and looks very magical.

Magnetic Spiral

Cut out the spiral card above.

Tell your audience that the spiral has strange magnetic powers. Rub it against your sleeve pretending to increase its magnetic energy.

Next place it on your head. Put your hand on the spiral and press hard against it. Now ask someone to grasp your wrist and try to lift your hand. Tell them that the magnetic energy is so strong that they will find it very difficult to do so.

Sure enough they will find it almost impossible to lift your 'magnetised' hand.

Finger Freezer

Cut out the snowflake card above.

Place your hand flat on a table with the middle finger folded under. Place the snowflake card under the ring finger as illustrated above.

All the other fingers may be lifted easily but when you try to lift the ring finger, you will find it very difficult.

Try this on a friend pretending that the snowflake momentarily freezes their finger.

Sneaky Snakes

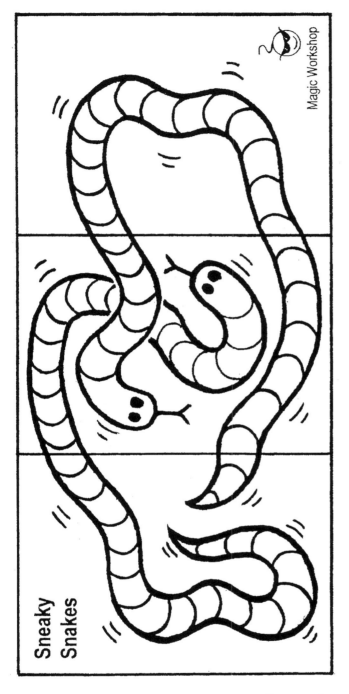

Cut out the three cards on the left.

Arrange the three cards on a table to show a picture of two long snakes.

Pick up the cards and, as you talk, secretly turn the middle card around.

Lay them on the table again and the picture will now show a very long snake and a short snake.

The Linking Rings

Cut out the three cards on the right.

Arrange the three cards on a table to show a magician holding two sets of rings. One set is linked and the other set is unlinked.

Pick up the cards and, as you talk, secretly turn the middle card around.

Lay them on the table again and the linked and unlinked sets will have changed places.

Peg the Picture Card

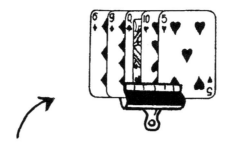

To make this trick you will need five playing cards, one of which should be a picture card, a two-inch bulldog clip and an ordinary spring clothes peg. Overlap the cards in a straight row with the picture card in the centre. Trap the cards within a bulldog clip as shown in the picture.

Hold the cards by the bulldog clip and display them face-up. Call attention to the position of the picture-card.

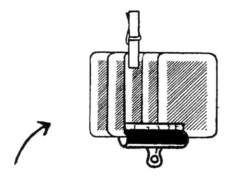

Turn the cards over and ask someone to mark the picture-card by fastening the peg over its end.

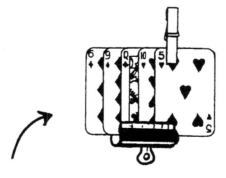

Now turn the cards face-up again and they will not believe their eyes. The peg will never appear to be where it should be.

Magic Choice

Cut out the two cards on the left.

Place the small prediction card, with the writing side downwards, on a table.

For the trick to work you must make someone choose the wand. This is achieved by asking someone to pick a number between one and six.

YOU WILL CHOOSE THE WAND

If they pick ONE	spell O,N,E, down from the top.
If they pick TWO	spell T,W,O, down from the top.
If they pick THREE	count 1,2,3, down from the top.
If they pick FOUR	count 1,2,3,4, up from the bottom.
If they pick FIVE	spell F,I,V,E, up from the bottom.
If they pick SIX	spell S,I,X, down from the top.

So you see, in this way, each number can bring them to 'choose' the wand.

To prove that you knew they would choose the wand, turn the prediction card over to reveal the message 'You will choose the wand'.

Tricky Tumblers

Use any three plastic tumblers. Place them on a table, middle one mouth upwards and the other two mouth down as shown above.

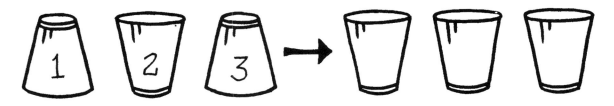

Demonstrate how with **three** moves only, you can finish with the three tumblers mouth upwards as above. Each move must consist of turning two tumblers at the same time, one in each hand.

Move one: Turn tumblers 1 and 2.

Move two: Turn tumblers 1 and 3.

Move three: Turn tumblers 1 and 2.

Challenge someone to do the same but before they begin, turn the centre tumbler mouth down. This puts the tumblers in a different starting position.

Now whichever way they attempt it, they will not end with all three tumblers mouth upwards. Even if they make the same moves as you demonstrated their tumblers will all be face downwards.

Lion to Girl

Cut out the picture above.

To turn the lion into a girl follow the folding instructions.

Birthday Cards

1	9	17	25
3	11	19	27
5	13	21	29
7	15	23	31

8	12	24	28
9	13	25	29
10	14	26	30
11	15	27	31

2	10	18	26
3	11	19	27
6	14	22	30
7	15	23	31

16	20	24	28
17	21	25	29
18	22	26	30
19	23	27	31

4	12	20	28
5	13	21	29
6	14	22	30
7	15	23	31

Cut out the five number cards above.

Ask a friend to think of their birthday. Show them the five cards, one by one, and have them tell you which cards have their birthday on them.

You are instantly able to tell them their birthday. All you have to do is silently add together the top left-hand corner numbers on the chosen cards.

The Square Puzzle

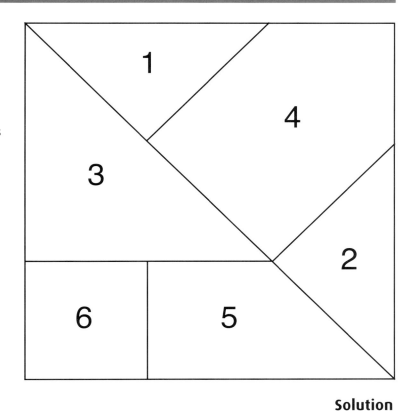

Cut carefully along the lines to make the six puzzle pieces.

Now try the following four puzzles without looking at the solutions.

Challenge   **Solution**

Level 1
Make a square from pieces 1 and 2 ————————————————→

Level 2
Make a square from pieces 1, 2 and 3 ————————————————→

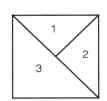

Level 3
Make a square from pieces 1, 2, 3, 4 and 5 ————————→

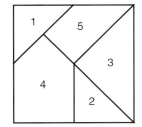

Level 4
Make a square from pieces 1, 2, 3, 4, 5 and 6 ————→

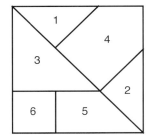

The Triangle Puzzle

Cut carefully along the lines to make the six puzzle pieces.

Now try the following four puzzles without looking at the solutions.

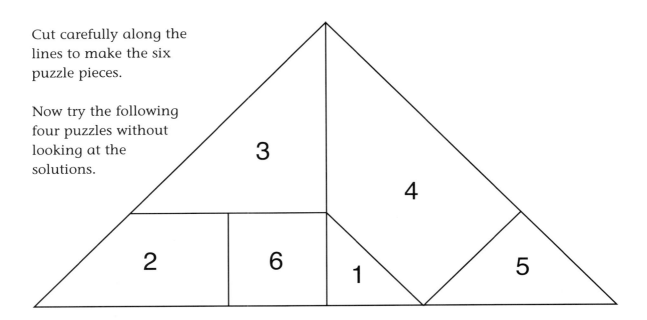

Challenge

Solution

Level 1
Make a triangle from pieces 1 and 2

Level 2
Make a triangle from pieces 1, 2 and 3

Level 3
Make a triangle from pieces 1, 2, 3, 4 and 5

Level 4
Make a triangle from pieces 1, 2, 3, 4, 5 and 6

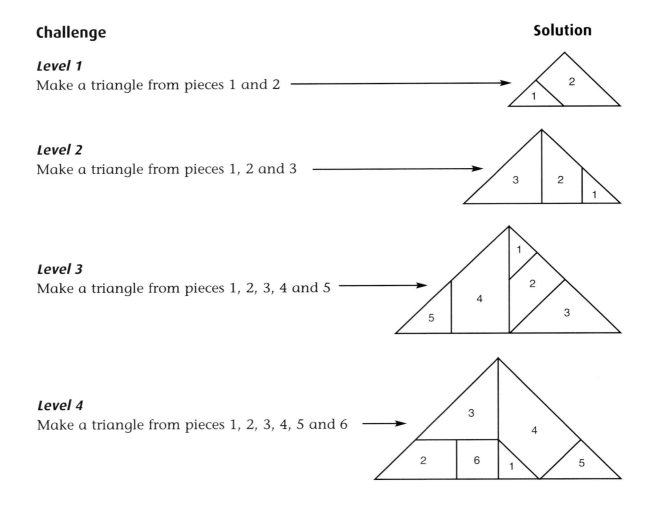

The Horse and Rider Puzzle

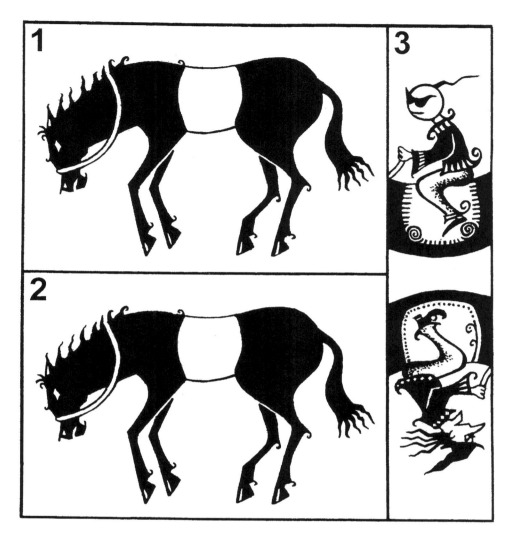

Carefully cut out the three cards. The challenge is to put the riders on their horses, in their propoer riding positions, without bending or cutting the cards.

Place card 1 and card 2 together so that the two horses are back to back.

Then place card 3 across the two cards to make two horses and riders, one of which is upside-down.

The Word Puzzles Sheet

Y R R U H ①	WHEATHER ②	.THAT'S ③	ONCE / A TIME ④
XQQQME ⑤	STAND / I ⑥	S I D E S I D E ⑦	VAD ERS ⑧
GETIT GETIT GETIT GETIT ⑨	PRO/MISE ⑩	ABCDEF GHIJKL MNOPQR STVW XYZ ⑪	MILONELION ⑫
CYCLE CYCLE CYCLE ⑬	ECNALG ⑭	LU CKY ⑮	You JUST me ⑯
LAL ⑰	AID← AID AID ⑱	.....ii ⑲	JACK ⑳

1. Hurry up
2. A bad spell of weather
3. That's beside the point
4. Once upon a time
5. Excuse me
6. I understand
7. Side by side
8. Space invaders
9. Forget it
10. Broken promise
11. Missing you
12. One in a million
13. Tricycle
14. Glance backwards
15. Lucky break
16. Just between you and me
17. All mixed up
18. First aid
19. Spots before the eyes
20. Jack in the box

Other Give-aways

As well as the workshop tricks, it is nice to include some extra items in the Give-away Magic Pack. This section contains a number of suitable items that I have included from time to time. The extra cost is very small and it further improves the quality of the pack. The items are of magical or associated interest and most kids enjoy them. You will, no doubt, come across other relevant items yourself.

Draw attention to the contents as you give out the pack. Explain about cutting out the *Certificate of Participation* and how it creates a magic wand by rolling it as illustrated. Read one or two riddles from the *Riddle Page* or do one of the simple tricks quickly. All this helps to add to the atmosphere and excitement of getting their own magic pack.

Riddle Page

- *What kind of dog likes air conditioning?*
  A Hot Dog

- *What is the most frightening kind of bee?*
  A zombie

- *What has six feet and can't move?*
  Two yards

- *What happened to the kitten that fell in love with the photocopier?*
  It became a copycat

- *Why didn't the dentist ask his secretary out on a date?*
  He was already taking out a tooth

- *What would cause a lot of trouble if it stopped smoking?*
  A chimney

- *What stays indoors no matter how many times you put it out?*
  The light

- *Who drives away all his customers?*
  A taxi driver

- *Why is a rubber band like a crocodile?*
  If you pull it too hard, it snaps

- *What is a magician's favourite nursery rhyme?*
  Trickery, Dickory, Dock

- *What is as large as an elephant but weighs nothing?*
  Its shadow

- *How did the boy have three hands on one arm?*
  He was wearing a watch

- *Why are giants popular?*
  Because people look up to them

- *How would you know if there was an elephant in your schoolbag?*
  You'd have trouble closing it up

- *What kind of hat do you wear on your leg?*
  A knee cap

- *Did you hear the joke about the pencil?*
  Never mind. There's no point!

- *What did the 'Dentist of the Year' get?*
  A little plaque

- *What does a policeman like on his toast?*
  Traffic jam

- *What side of a chicken has the most feathers?*
  The outside

- *What does a magician say when he takes a picture?*
  Focus Pocus

A Sweet Trick

What you need

A baseball cap and a sweet.

What to do

Put the sweet on a table and cover it with the baseball cap. Bet your friends that you can eat the sweet without lifting the cap.

Here's how you do it

Go under the table and make eating sounds with your mouth. Then come up smiling and licking your lips. When they lift the cap to check your claim, quickly pick up the sweet and eat it.

You didn't lift the cap, **they** did! So you see, you did succeed in eating the sweet without lifting the cap!

The Shoelace Trick

What you need

Three shoelaces.

What to do

Show your friends the three shoelaces.

Take two of the shoelaces and tie them together with a knot.

Now challenge your friends to put the third shoelace between the other two without breaking them or undoing the knot.

Solution

It's very simple. All you have to do is tie the third shoelace to the ends of the other two so that you have a circle of three shoelaces (as shown below). Any one of them is now between the other two!

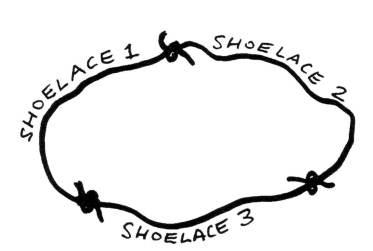

Which Hand?

What you need

A coin.

What to do

Give your friend the coin to hold. Explain to him that while you are out of the room, he is to raise the hand holding the coin up to his forehead while counting sixty seconds. He must then lower his hand and call you back into the room.

Using your incredible mental powers (?) you study his two closed fists and correctly guess which hand contains the coin.

How did you know?

The hand that holds the object will be slightly whiter than the other hand, due to the fact that it was held up, and so its blood vessels are less dilated.

Maths Wiz

Think of a number between 1 and 10

Multiply it by 2

Add 4 to it

Divide it by 2

Subtract the first number you thought of

Your answer is 2

Magical Anagrams

Here are some mixed up magical words.
Juggle around the letters to find the proper spellings.

NAWD

IEDC

LEPLS

KIRCT

CIGMA

EESTRC

BARTIB

SLOINUIL

GANICAMI

CRRAAAAABBD

The Answers

WAND
DICE
SPELL
TRICK
MAGIC
SECRET
RABBIT
ILLUSION
MAGICIAN
ABRACADABRA

Conclusion

You could say that presenting the Magic Workshop is quite an amount of work. You could equally say that it's a whole lot of fun. I certainly have had a lot of fun with it over the years and I know that you too will enjoy presenting it to your groups. As the saying goes 'if you enjoy your job you'll never work a day'. I have travelled around to numerous schools doing art, magic and games with kids of all ages for many years. It certainly wasn't all effortless but it was an incredible amount of fun. I really haven't worked a day in all those years! Indeed, sometimes the kids think that what I do with them is not my real job and they often ask me 'Tommy what job do you actually work at?' Cheeky or what!

To find out about other suitable tricks to use in your Magic Workshops and to keep in contact for future developments on the concept, log onto my web site at:

www.gamesandmagic.com

The book ends here but the magic, I hope, will continue. I would be delighted to receive your comments regarding this book and any thoughts you may have on The Magic Workshop. You can email me on:

info@gamesandmagic.com

In the meantime, may I wish you fun, laughter and magic – in both your group-work and in your life!

Good luck and happy magic workshopping,

Thomas Moloney